A Gentleman's GUIDE TO Toasting

A
Gentleman's
GUIDE TO
Toasting

Edited by
Dave Fulmer
Gentleman Jack Toastmaster
Jack Daniel Distillery

Oxmoor
HOUSE®

Library of Congress Catalog Number: 90-62244
ISBN: 0-8487-1057-6
Manufactured in the United States of America
First Edition
Executive Editor: Nancy Fitzpatrick
Production Manager: Jerry Higdon
Associate Production Manager: Rick Litton
Art Director: Bob Nance
Editor: Rebecca Brennan
Book Design: Bob Nance
Production Assistant: Theresa L. Beste
Research Assistant: Linda Denton

A Gentleman's Guide to Toasting
Author: Dave Fulmer
Contributing Writer: Nelson Eddy

Second toast on page 30 excerpted from *10,000 Jokes, Toasts and Stories*
by Lewis and Faye Copeland Eds., © 1930, 1940 by Lewis and Faye
Copeland, © 1965 Doubleday, a division of Bantam Doubleday Dell
Publishing Group, Incorporated. Used by permission of the publisher.

Toast on page 67 from the movie *The Thin Man* © 1934 Metro-
Goldwyn-Mayer Corporation, Ren. 1961 Metro-Goldwyn-Mayer Inc.

Toasts on page 75 from *The Pleasure of Your Company* by Pat Ross, © Pat
Ross, 1989. All Rights Reserved. Reprinted by permission of Viking
Penguin, a division of Penguin Books USA Inc.

Special thanks to Paul Dickson, author of *Toasts: The Complete Book of the
Best Toasts, Sentiments, Blessings, Curses, and Graces.*

Gentleman Jack Rare Tennessee Whiskey
40% Alcohol by Volume (80 Proof)
Distilled and Bottled by Jack Daniel Distillery,
Lem Motlow, Proprietor, Lynchburg (Pop. 361), Tenn.

To my friends,

Friends we are today,
And friends we'll always be—
For I am wise to you,
And you can see through me.

Contents

Introduction

THERE ARE THOSE UNIVERSAL GESTURES THAT have A rare magic to lift us and mark the simplest of moments as special—a tender kiss, a warm ovation, and a well-offered toast.

Of the three, the toast is the most mysterious. A toast is all at once a poem, a public prayer, a proverb, a secret sentiment, a roast, a bit of wit, and a veritable verbal badge of social facility. Which is to say, a good toast is hard to find. And so this gentle guide.

The civilized and genteel art of toast-giving is, appropriately, as old as civilization itself. And like most symbols of civilization—Venus de Milo, Aristotelian logic, and wrestling—toasting goes back to the ancient Greeks.

In the days before tamperproof packaging, the Greeks began the practice of drinking to one another's health and welfare. It was a good faith gesture designed to excuse the nasty Greek habit of spiking the punch with poison.

Later, the Romans refined the custom by improving upon the palatability of the potables of the period. The Romans proved their good taste by discovering that a piece of burnt bread—toast—placed in a goblet seemed to mellow the flavor of the wine. It was the char on the chunk of bread that did it.

And that, dear friends, is how charcoal-mellowing of fine Tennessee Whiskey was born. Well, maybe . . . but, more to the point of this book, that's how the "toast" came to be part of the social imbiber's vocabulary today.

Since the Greeks, gracious toasts have raised the spirits of gentle folk around the globe. Today the cultured of every culture have developed their own favorite phrases of praise to accompany the clink of the glass among friends.

What follows here is a guide to the gentlemanly art of toast-giving. Included are a few introductory tips, suggested etiquette, some passing anecdotes, and an illustrated collection of a few of the most beloved toasts.

So let's begin with a toast by the French philosopher André Gide to writers, speakers, and all aspirant toast-makers:

Everything worth saying has already been said—
But since no one was listening,
It's necessary to repeat it.

Shall we drink to it?

Guide to Gracious Toast-Giving

I WOULD PREFER TO LEAVE THE SUBJECT, MANNER, method, and mode of your toast-making up to you. But in this modern age of guides on everything from fly-tying to bow-tying, résumé-writing to social-wrong-righting, gentle folks are in constant search of good advice.

There's a lot of American know-how showing Americans how-to.

So I'm offering my advice on toast-giving with the peace of mind that the American appetite for knowing the rules is second only to the American passion for breaking the rules.

Remember, rules are for common men. When uncommon folks break the rules, it's called style.

⁂

- *Be Eloquent, Whimsical, and Witty.* Tough assignment, but try. Toasting is not for the thick of tongue or faint of phrase. The best way to achieve all three is to learn from the examples that follow in this book. Remember, it's impossible to put your foot in your mouth if you keep the latter closed.

- *Be Simple.* Simply put, the simplest toast is often the most sincere.

- *Be Yourself.* The best words, witticisms, and stories are your own. A toast is toastier if it's original. The toasts that follow are for your inspiration and learning. But remember what I said about breaking the rules.

- *Be Brief.* Brevity is the soul of wit, not to mention the heart of hospitality. The well-turned toast is terse. As the great Toastmaster General of the United States, George Jessel observed: "If you haven't struck oil in your first three minutes, stop boring!"

- *Be Prepared.* A toast is a public speech in miniature. As such, the best toast is well prepared and painstakingly practiced. If you want to sound spontaneous, rehearse first.

- *Be Done.* Lead your audience gracefully into your conclusion by using any or all of the generally accepted toast-terminating gestures: Finish with a verbal flourish, raise your glass, "clink" with a partner, and take a sip.

Toast Etiquette
&
Protocol

What follows is a list of things "they" generally say should and shouldn't be done when giving a toast.

I've never had a satisfactory explanation as to whom "they" are. But I include this list just so you know what you're doing when "they" get upset because you're not doing it.

- Don't raise your glass or drink when you're the one being toasted. It's like applauding for yourself. If you're uncomfortable not doing anything, as soon as the toast is completed, raise your glass and say, "Thank you. And here's to all of you."

- Don't toast the guest of honor before the host has the opportunity.

- If seated at a table, stand when offering your toast.

- Avoid signaling for quiet by rapping on a glass with a spoon. The results could be shattering.

- Although the superstitious consider it bad luck, it is far more polite to join in a toast with a non-alcoholic beverage or even an empty glass than to refuse to participate.

- Refrain from smashing your glass in the fireplace as the heat of the fire may melt the glass to the brick.

Etiquette
for
Special Occasions

People are searching for meaning in their lives . . . in one sentence or less. The toast is a communications vehicle for our time. With the tersest of toasts, a meandering social gathering can be compacted into a simple sentence that sums it all up. Raise the significance of special occasions by raising a toast.

Here's some suggested etiquette to aid you.

• At an engagement party, the engagement is formally announced to those in attendance by the father of the bride in an appropriate toast.

• At a wedding reception in which a meal is served, toasts are traditionally offered once everyone has been seated and served their drinks. At a standing reception, toasts are offered after everyone has gone through the receiving line and drinks have been served.

• With large weddings, it is best to engage in toast-making at the more informal rehearsal dinner than during the reception.

• At either the wedding reception or rehearsal dinner, toasts are generally offered to the bridal couple beginning with the best man. The groom responds with a toast of thanks. Other toasts to the couple may follow in any order deemed appropriate, generally:

1. Fathers, beginning with the father of the bride
2. Mothers, beginning with the mother of the bride
3. Groom to the bride
4. Bride to the groom

This order may also be used at anniversary dinners.

• At a christening luncheon or tea, toasts are generally offered to the child in the following order:

1. Godparents
2. Parents
3. Siblings
4. Guests

Libations

Toasting is a form of spiritual communication. And when toasting, as with all communication, the medium carries the message.

The only rule regarding choice of your liquid medium is what's appropriate. Toasts during weddings, anniversaries, and romantic moments certainly deserve a more elegant libation than the informal landing-of-the-fifteen-pound-pike toast. Having a taste for the appropriate potable is part of the art of toast-giving.

The four universally accepted toasting libations are champagne, wine, whiskey, and beer. Of the four, I have always had a fond taste for fine whiskey.

The toasts that follow have been tested several times by the compiler raising a 4½-ounce brandy snifter sporting a splash of Gentleman Jack Rare Tennessee Whiskey. I will not guarantee that any of the toasts included in this volume will hoist as well with any lesser beverage.

I prefer a brandy snifter when tasting and toasting with a fine whiskey for both functional and aesthetic reasons. First, its shape is designed to hold the nose or aroma of the beverage. And smell is an essential element of proper whiskey sipping. Secondly, a snifter's urbane design puts one in the proper frame of mind for spouting a poetic tribute.

> Here's to the snifter stem
> Which raises the spirit
> And the heart of man.
> Here's to the snifter bowl
> Which I cup in my palm
> To warm the spirit like a toasty balm.

See what I mean . . .

Toasts
for
All
Occasions

When friends with other friends contrive
To make their glasses clink,
Then not one sense of all the five
Is absent from a drink.
For touch and taste and smell and sight
Evolve in pleasant round,
And when the flowing cups unite
We thrill to sense of sound.
Folly to look on wine? Oh, fie
On what teetotalers think . . .
There's always five good reasons why
Good fellows like to drink.

—E.B.A.
1937 bar guide

Here's to politicians.
The distiller's true friend.
For wherever you find four politicians together,
You're sure to find a fifth.

The above toast is a favorite used by the Jack Daniel Distillery tour guides, who have been known to offer it up in honor of any and all political, religious, social, civic, and professional groups by quick change of the first line. —Ed.

To the thirst that is yet to come.
—*Irish*

Toasts
of
Congratulations

My heartfelt congratulations to the gentle people of Lynchburg, Tennessee. Today you are recognized around the world for your good taste and the spirits you raise.

—JACK DANIEL

The above toast is attributed to Jack Daniel and has been passed down through the years by word-of-mouth. The old story goes that Mr. Daniel offered the toast at a special party in Lynchburg celebrating his Gold Medal victory at the 1904 St. Louis World's Fair. Mr. Jack Daniel's whiskey was one of twenty entered from around the world in a prestigious exhibition and tasting. And it was the only whiskey awarded a Gold Medal and honored by an international panel of judges as the world's best. The gentleman distiller commemorated his World's Fair Gold Medal with a special bottling in a decorative decanter and a special toast of thanks. —Ed.

Here's to your promotion.
Nothing succeeds like success.

In your new position may you be
Thick-skinned,
Level headed,
Sure-footed,
Even-handed,
Nimble-fingered,
Sharp-eyed,
Open-minded,
Quick-witted,
Smooth-tongued,
And humble . . .
If at all possible.
—LINDA DENTON

To your recent success and promotion.
I've known some of the best.
I've known some of the worst.
And, believe me,
You have to be one of the most.

If at first you don't succeed,
Adjust your goals.

A wise man once said that every successful
Enterprise requires three men—a dreamer,
A businessman, and an S.O.B.
Here's to you.

Toasts
for
Special
Occasions

Weddings
&
Anniversaries

To my daughter, the bride:
May the first day of your new life together
Be filled with as much joy, wonder
And possibility
As the first day of our life together.

Here's to my mother-in-law's daughter,
And here's to her father-in-law's son;
And here's to the vows we've just taken,
And the life we've just begun.

Marriage: A community consisting of
A master,
A mistress and
Two slaves—
Making in all, two.
—AMBROSE BIERCE

May your wedding days be few
And your anniversaries many.

Grow old with me!
The best is yet to be,
The last of life,
For which, the first is made.
—ROBERT BROWNING

May we be loved by those we love.

Christenings

Every baby born into the world
Is a finer one than the last.
—CHARLES DICKENS
Nicholas Nickleby

We haven't all had the good fortune to be ladies;
We haven't all been generals, or poets,
Or statesmen;
But when the toast works down to the babies,
We stand on common ground.
—SAMUEL L. CLEMENS

A baby will make love stronger,
Days shorter, nights longer,
Bankroll smaller, home happier,
Clothes shabbier,
The past forgotten,
And the future worth living for.

Birthdays

May you live to be a hundred years
With one extra year to repent.
—*Traditional Irish Toast*

As we travel through life,
May we live well on the road.

May you live all the days of your life.
—JONATHAN SWIFT

May you live forever
And die happy.
—L. R. FULMER,
*Methodist preacher,
teetotaler, and the editor's father*

Toasts
to
the
Holidays

Thanksgiving

Here's to the feast that has plenty of meat
And very little tablecloth.

Bless the Lord, O my soul.
He causeth the grass to grow for the cattle,
And herb for the service of man:
That he may bring forth food out of the earth;
And wine that maketh glad the heart of man,
And oil to make his face to shine,
And bread which strengtheneth man's heart.
—*Psalms 104:1, 14-15*

Christmas

To the Spirit of Christmas,
May peace on Earth and goodwill toward men
Never be as hard to come by
As fine whiskey.
—JACK DANIEL

Legend has it that Jack Daniel, the gentleman distiller of Lynchburg, offered the above toast at Christmastime during the Civil War. The hardships of the war threatened his distillery business and whiskey was scarce. —Ed.

Here's to us all—
God bless us every one!
—CHARLES DICKENS
Tiny Tim's toast,
A CHRISTMAS CAROL

May you savor the gentle spirit
Of this holiday season.

Toasts
to
Politics
&
War

To peace and friendship among all people.
—PRESIDENT JIMMY CARTER
June 25, 1979

Allow me to raise a glass to the work
that has been done,
the work that remains to be done.
And let us also toast the art of
friendly persuasion,
the home of peace with freedom,
the hope of holding out
for a better way of settling things.
—PRESIDENT RONALD REAGAN
TO GENERAL SECRETARY MIKHAIL GORBACHEV
Moscow, May 30, 1989

In a classic display of political one-upmanship, the British Ambassador, the French Minister, and American emissary Benjamin Franklin offered the following round of toasts while dining at Versailles. —Ed.

British Ambassador:
[To] George III, who, like the sun in its meridian, spreads a luster throughout and enlightens the world.

French Minister:
[To] the illustrious Louis XVI, who, like the moon, sheds his mild and benignant rays on and influences the globe.

Benjamin Franklin:
[To] George Washington, commander of the American armies, who, like Joshua of old, commanded the sun and the moon to stand still, and they obeyed him.

War

Here's mud in your eye!

This toast was very popular during World War I, a war which was fought in the trenches. The toast originated during the opening of the American West as a departing blessing on farmers heading westward. —Ed.

To the enemies of our country!
May they have cobweb breeches,
A porcupine saddle,
A hard-trotting horse,
And an eternal journey.
—*American Revolutionary War toast*

To long lives and short wars.
—COLONEL POTTER
M*A*S*H

Toasts
to
Ladies
&
Gentlemen

Ladies

Here's to the maiden of bashful fifteen;
Here's to the widow of fifty;
Here's to the flaunting, extravagant queen,
And here's to the housewife that's thrifty.
Let the toast pass;
Drink to the lass;
I'll warrant she'll prove an excuse for the glass.
—RICHARD BRINSLEY SHERIDAN
The School for Scandal

❧

During the seventeenth century, drinking a toast referred to drinking to a lady. An explanation of this practice was written by Sir Richard Steele and appeared in the Tatler, *June 4, 1709:*

> *It happened that on a publick day a celebrated beauty of those times was in the cross bath, and one of the crowd of her admirers took a glass of the water in which the fair one stood, and drank her health to the company. There was in the place a gay fellow, half fuddled, who offered to jump in, and swore, though he liked not the liquor, he would have the toast. He was opposed in his resolution; yet this whim gave foundation to the present honor which is done to the lady we mention in our liquor, who has ever since been called toast.*

From this, celebrated people became known as the "toast of the town." —Ed.

Let us have wine and women,
Mirth and laughter,
Sermons and soda-water the day after.
—LORD BYRON
Don Juan

It gives me great pleasure.
—GEORGE BERNARD SHAW

George Bernard Shaw offered the above toast during a fashionable English dinner party at which it was the custom of the host to select both the giver and subject of the toast. In an apparent attempt to tongue-tie the great literary lion, the host selected the subject of sex—an unmentionable in society at the turn of the century. Shaw responded simply and to the point. A lesson for all who aspire to offer toasts. —Ed.

She is mine own,
And I as rich in having such a jewel,
As twenty seas, if all their sands were pearl,
The water nectar and the rocks pure gold.
—WILLIAM SHAKESPEARE

What, sir, would the people of the earth
Be without woman?
They would be scarce, sir, almighty scarce.
—Samuel L. Clemens

Gentlemen

Here's to the man who is wisest and best
Here's to the man who with judgment is blest.
Here's to the man who's as smart as can be—
I drink to the man who agrees with me!

To men:
You can't live with 'em;
And you can't shoot 'em.

May every man be
What he thinks himself to be.

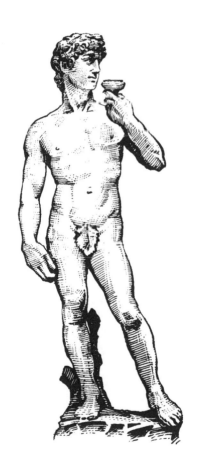

Toasts
for
Sporting
Occasions

Here's to the lass who serves the drinks,
And to the man who picks up the check.
And here's to the Georgia Bulldogs and
To Hell with Georgia Tech.
—LEWIS GRIZZARD

Lewis Grizzard is a nationally syndicated columnist
and author of numerous bestselling books. —Ed.

Here's to the honest golfer:
To long drives,
Wide fairways,
Short putts,
And lost scorecards.

To golf, the most difficult of sports to master,
Which may be why golf spelled backwards is flog.

To Washington,
First in war,
First in peace,
And last in the American League.

Toasts in Memoriam

A prayer to the gods I may and must offer,
That they will prosper my journey
From this to the other world . . .
—SOCRATES
(over a glass of hemlock)

Now let us sit and drink and make us merry,
And afterward we will his body bury.
—GEOFFREY CHAUCER
The Canterbury Tales

From the earth we were formed,
To the earth we return . . .
And in between we garden.
—NELSON EDDY

Now, my friends, if I may propose a little toast:

Let us eat, drink and be merry,
For tomorrow . . . we die.
—WILLIAM POWELL
The Thin Man

William Powell offers the above toast as Detective Nick Charles to his dinner guests (each a murder suspect) in the movie The Thin Man. *—Ed.*

Toasts
of
Good
Cheer

Life

May the road rise to meet you,
May the wind be always at your back,
The sun shine warm upon your face,
The rain fall soft upon your fields,
And until we meet again
May God hold you in the hollow of His hand.
—*Traditional Irish Toast*

Let your boat of life be light
Packed with only what you need—
A homely home and simple pleasures,
One or two friends, worth the name,
Someone to love and someone to love you,
A cat, a dog, and a pipe or two,
Enough to eat and enough to wear,
And a little more than enough to drink . . .
For thirst is a dangerous thing.
—JEROME K. JEROME
Three Men in a Boat

Cool breeze,
Warm fire,
Full moon,
Easy chair,
Empty plates,
Soft words,
Sweet songs,
Tall tales,
Short sips,
Long life.
—JOHN EGERTON

I drink to the days that are!
—WILLIAM MORRIS

Here's hoping that you live forever
And mine is the last voice you hear.
—WILLARD SCOTT

Friendship

Here's champagne to our real friends,
And real pain to our sham friends.

I've traveled many a highway
I've walked for many a mile
Here's to the people who made my day
To the people who waved and smiled.
—Tom T. Hall

May we never see an old friend
With a new face.

Hospitality

I thank you for your welcome, which was cordial
And your cordial, which was welcome.

A toast to our host
And a song from the short and tall of us,
May he live to be
The guest of all of us!

Prosperity

May you live as long as you want
And may you never want as long as you live.

May bad fortune follow you all your days
And never catch up with you.

Here's to your good health,
And your family's good health,
And may you all live long and prosper.
—WASHINGTON IRVING
Rip Van Winkle

Esperanto	Je zia sano
Chinese	Kan bei
French	Santé
German	Prosit
Irish	Slainte
Italian	Salute
Japanese	Kampai
Russian	Na zdorovia
Scottish	Slainte
Swedish	Skoal
Spanish	Salud

From their ancient Greek origins, toasts have long enjoyed an important place in international diplomacy. The ancient custom of drinking to one's health was a means of assuring a visiting dignitary that his beverage was not spiked with poison, an early form of political dirty tricks. —Ed.

To temperance . . . in moderation.

—LEM MOTLOW
Proprietor of the Jack Daniel Distillery
Lynchburg(Pop. 361), Tennessee